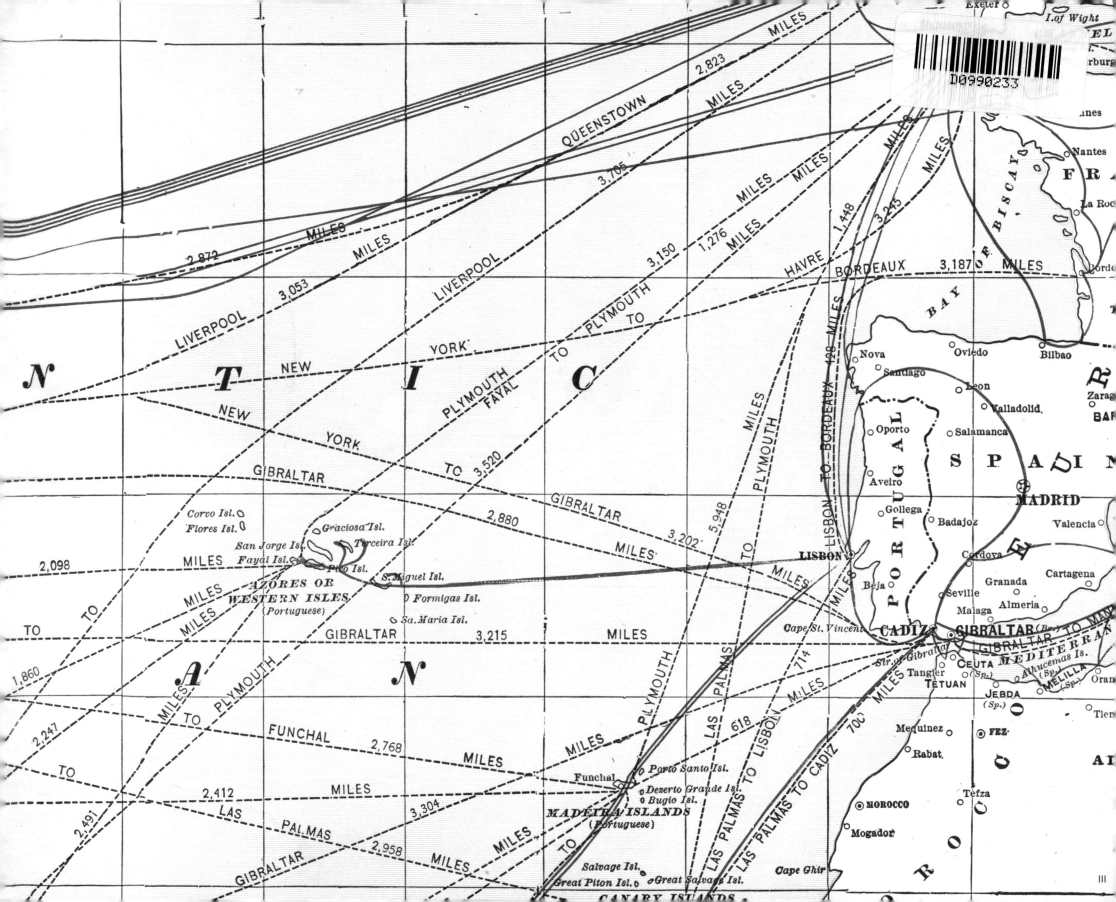

PICTURE

Amelia

THE MOTION PICTURE

Introduction by Mira Nair
Foreword by Hilary Swank

Amelia Earhart, 1933

IN HER COMPANY

Mira in Bhubaneswar, 1969

WHEN I WAS THIRTEEN years old in Bhubaneswar, the new capital of the remote eastern state of Orissa, the first commercial air service came to town. One Fokker Friendship from Calcutta would land each day, and I would rush out through the tall grasses surrounding the temples to stand by the barbed-wire fence of the airfield, watching the plane land and lift off. I knew one day I would be on that plane.

Decades later, when I was asked to make a film on Amelia Earhart, I felt an affinity with her because she too came from a tiny place—Atchison, Kansas—a town like Bhubaneswar. She too dreamed of borderless horizons, of seeing wild places, like Morocco, Spain, and Angola; she was intoxicated with life.

Quite honestly, I wanted to be in her company.

Amelia came from good breeding but not much money; yet she got where she wanted to go with confidence, focus, and pluck. She was truly a world child, resisting the insularity of turn-of-the-century Middle America. A woman who channeled her courage to follow her dream, for the fun of it, as she would say, yet she harnessed her energies to be hugely useful to others. It astonished me to learn that the passenger flights, which we take so much for granted today, were actually promoted, and in many ways made possible, by Amelia and Gene Vidal. Lanky, androgynous, and elegant, she was unafraid to be herself, and was a great believer in fun. Without pomposity or self-importance, Amelia was secure enough to quietly create her own path, whether in marriage or in making record-breaking flights. In this sense, she defined what it is to be modern.

In Hilary Swank, I found the spiritual embodiment of Amelia. The physical resemblance was so uncanny that it allowed us to slip in and out of newsreels of the real Amelia and constructed ones of Hilary as her. Also a daredevil, Hilary was close to getting her flying license as she prepared for the film. One night as we set off for a weekend after a grueling week of work, I will never forget the image of her running on the tarmac toward the plane, clicking her heels high in the air, exultant with the joy of it.

In some ways, thanks to her relationship with George Putnam, her husband, publisher, and manager, Amelia was the first celebrity to become something of a commodity herself. So there is much of her available in newsreels, photography, advertising, even cookbook recipes. Her image was used to endorse everything from luggage to clothing and cameras. Yet I was struck by her goofy humility in the face of her accolades and fame; her expression seems always humble and observant, as if she surrendered with good grace to all the hoopla—all so she could fly.

I began to visualize the film as a study of Amelia's striving for balance between the ecstasy of the sky and the responsibility of the earth. We filmed the story chronologically, but it wasn't until we turned the film on its head, beginning with Amelia's final flight and having her guide us back and forth between present, past, and future, that I found the voice of my Amelia. The film became about memory and dreams and ellipsis. Once again, flying had given us the key.

After months of retracing her steps, understanding her style, seeing signs of her legacy everywhere, my film family and I began to build her world. As always, authenticity became our treasure. We built the vintage planes to exaction, aviation enthusiasts all over the world offered us their lovingly burnished planes, we took months to carefully build the grass landing strip from which the Electra would take off for the last time. The great seascapes of Newfoundland where Amelia had actually taken off on her earliest flights across the Atlantic were exactly where we went to film the Friendship flight; to create the final flight of the Electra, South Africa became our base from where

we built the circle. Nelson Mandela's home area of the Transkei became our Papua New Guinea, in Nadeni we built the Askia Tomb of Mali and the Dumdum aerodrome of my childhood in Calcutta, Namibia became Sudan, the ocean around the Cape of Good Hope became the Pacific that swallowed her.

I saw her ending as returning to the ether she came from, at home in the sky where she belonged.

Mira Nair

BECOMING AMELIA

THERE ARE TIMES when incredible people resonate so profoundly with us, that they impact the way we live our lives. For me, Amelia Earhart was one of those people. She was acutely aware of the dangers of exploring uncharted waters, but was never afraid to do so. I know it's a cliché, but appropriate in this instance—Amelia was ahead of her time. She took premed classes at Columbia University, and upon reflection of her first flight as a passenger, she exclaimed, "I knew I had to fly."

Early in her life, Amelia kept a scrapbook of newspaper clippings about women she admired, who had succeeded in careers that were dominated by men. Coincidentally, she herself became an inspiration for many young women to achieve their dreams. She is a defining symbol for women that there are no limits.

I am honored and humbled to be part of a film that brings her incredible story to life. Amelia's journey has and will continue to inspire people of every generation. As Amelia once said, "I am quite aware of the hazards. Women must try to do things as men have tried. When they fail, their failure must be but a challenge to others."

Hilary Swank

Amelia in front of a map
showing her route, ca. 1937

SEARCHING FOR AMELIA

WHEN I WAS A CHILD, I lived next door to the public library. And spent much of my time there. In the stacks. The stacks marked, GIRL'S BOOKS. Florence Nightingale, Clara Barton, Amelia Earhart. As a good Catholic girl, I understood the why of lives of sacrifice and service. But this woman who flew around in the sky? Why? I did not get it. As far as I was concerned Amelia Earhart could stay in the stacks. Years later film director Mira Nair asked me to come aboard her project about the life of the iconic aviatrix. Always having wanted to work with Mira, I signed on. Figured it would be a fairly easy gig. Character work was my specialty as a screenwriter. Especially crafting characters based on fact. My first task would be to "find" the true-life Amelia. Her soul. The wound she tap-danced around. Every memorable film character has one. And then to use that scar to layer the character Hilary Swank would portray on the screen. My search for Amelia Earhart commenced. After slogging my way through most all of the thirty-eight books written about the woman, I began thinking it would be easier to "find" her at the bottom of the Pacific. I was still nine years old, in the stacks, wondering, Why? Then a stroke of good fortune. Gore Vidal, who as a child knew Amelia, was kind enough to spend an afternoon with Mira, Hilary, and me. To share his memories. It wasn't so much what he said about Amelia, but how he said it. With a definite tinge of sadness. The first tumbler in the padlock clicked. Then there was the photograph. Amelia holding a bouquet of flowers, standing on the steps of the Massachusetts State House with other celebrated people of the day. She appeared lost behind the ever-present smile. As if she didn't belong. Insecure and alien. I went back to the research material, looked at it through a different prism. Finally, the dots began to connect. Answers to the whys. The why behind her fierce desire to fly. To break records. To fly higher and further. To take risks. The most famous, most admired woman in the world believed she was not good enough. As a pilot, not skilled enough. As an advocate for women's equality, not effective enough. As a wife, not devoted and loving enough. And as a woman, never attractive enough. My search for Amelia would continue throughout the writing process. But I was finally on the runway and some of the fog had lifted.

Anna Hamilton Phelan
WRITER

FOR THE FUN OF IT

AMELIA EARHART flew for the fun of it, and I like to think I design for the same reason.

Fun means designing a period film with a sweeping scope, fabricating sets all over the world. It also eans getting to design the world of a daredevil, a feminist whose aviation accomplishments not only changed the world but also whose image is so iconic, so cool, that almost eighty years after her disappearance her image is used to sell hip khaki clothing.

Amelia Earhart as advertising icon (a.k.a. shill) was a theme present in the film, too—one that was exploited by a highly stylized montage design built and shot on the soundstage in Toronto.

Down the hall in the construction shop, carpentry, welding, and scenic crews spent weeks reconstructing Amelia's planes inch by perfect inch—the orange canvas-walled Friendship and the bright red Vega. It was humbling to realize just how primitive these airplanes actually were back in the day; the scripted scene of Amelia tumbling out the door of the Friendship could now be more graphically understood.

As for my design inspiration, the first image that I showed to Mira was a two-year-old illustration from *The New Yorker* magazine of one of Jenny Holzer's art installations featuring an airplane flying over the Hudson towing a banner which read WHAT YOU FEAR OVERTAKES YOU. The image felt emotionally correct for Amelia, and the image and truism became almost a mascot for the art department. The plane and banner were, with the help of Wojciech Zielinski and his visual effects team, included as a design element in the Powder Puff Derby set.

The second image I showed to Mira was *Portrait of a Young Woman*, painted in 1935 by art-deco inspired painter Meredith Frampton. It influenced both the color palette and design of *Amelia*, as did other painters, such as Tamara de Lempicka, Jean Dupas, and Imre Goth.

These early Holzer and Frampton images were harbingers: from this point in prep, Mira and I poured over hundreds of fine art images, books, photographs, and research visuals to define and refine the look of the film. It was somewhat like the perpetual shoveling of coal into a steamship oven, feeding the beasts.

Art-deco and cubist painters were main influences for me, but there were as many determinants as there were scenes. Studying Buddhist cave paintings from Dunhuang Province in China helped design the wall murals for Amelia's Los Angeles home, fueling myself with Henri Rousseau helped produce the wallpaper in Gore's Connecticut bedroom set, and the African tomb, with its shapely wood shafts, were inspired by books on Timbuktu.

The design canvas for *Amelia* was vast: from creating New York offices, Connecticut homes, and a variety of East Coast sets in Toronto, to constructing a Welsh seaport and Irish fields in Nova Scotia, then crossing the ocean to design Los Angeles, New Guinea, and Saharan and Western Africa sets in South Africa.

It feels like sometimes we moved mountains to make *Amelia*, but during the trip we flew over some great ones, too.

Stephanie Carroll
PRODUCTION DESIGNER

Amelia teaching students, 1933

CAPTURING AMELIA

TO BE A *STILLS* PHOTOGRAPHER on a *motion* picture can be a strange and sometimes frustrating pursuit. After all, the full sum of resources and energy are expended for the purpose of creating the motion picture. That means the film camera (and usually more than one) has all the best angles—and rightly so. That being said, I never once felt like an interloper in the world of *Amelia* and was consistently afforded every possible opportunity to photograph as widely and freely as possible by the extremely talented and experienced crew and cast.

The world of *Amelia* was truly a visual feast; rich with fantastic locations in both Canada and South Africa, stunning period wardrobe and set design, amazing vintage aircraft, and dynamic performances. Every day brought fresh vistas, ideas, and experiences.

I can only hope that the resulting photographs do some justice to the images and ideas as expressed in the film, and to the countless hours of incredibly hard work done by hundreds of contributors. All for the sake, as director Mira Nair once so eloquently described it, our mutual devotion to "the sacred frame."

Ken Woroner
PHOTOGRAPHER

OUR LADY OF THE SKIES

SEVENTY-ONE YEARS after Amelia Earhart's disappearance, I received an e-mail which read "...you own one of the few surviving Electras, what about having it play the role of Amelia's aircraft in our coming film?" The Electra is a masterpiece, an art-deco, civilized, sophisticated airplane whose wings are filled with magical potential. Only a dozen remain. We were asked to bring the Electra from its home in France to the set in South Africa.

Our sixty-seven-year-old Electra had a long and storied history of service to king and country, but at the time she was inside a hangar, engineless, propellerless, and suffering from a host of other problems. We had four months to fix her, and organized the adventure into three parts: ferry flight down along the west coast of Africa, filming flights across South Africa, and return ferry flight along the eastern coast.

With two and a half weeks left before shooting was to begin, we lifted off from Annemasse airfield. After a host of problems involving paying for gas, landing fees, hotels, as well as the quality of gas and, most importantly, the weather, and a three-day detainment in Equatorial New Guinea (on a trumped-up charge of violating airspace), the exhausted crew landed in Capetown at the last possible moment.

During the three weeks of shooting, our lady of the skies became a part of the cast. Hilary Swank behaved as if she and the aircraft really were Amelia and her Electra. During the afternoon of her birthday, Hilary was locked into the cockpit. It was hot and smelled of gasoline. After some time Hilary said, in a low voice, "When I was a little girl, I wanted to be a film actress. I really wanted that. And now it's my birthday, and here I am, a film actress." A happy moment for us all.

After filming was over, and the flight home was plagued with even more weather and bureaucratic problems, the Electra landed at its base near Geneva.

To cure the after-filming blues, I went through some photos in Purdue University's Amelia Earhart archives. I knew my dad, an aviator in his own right, had met Amelia in Dakar, Senegal, just weeks before she disappeared. But suddenly, it all became clear to me as I discovered three photos labeled "Amelia at the Aero Club dinner, Dakar." They showed Amelia, Fred Noonan, and my dad standing ready for a banquet.

It was the proper ending to a wonderful adventure. Fate had indeed organized it all in grand style.

Bernard Chabbert
PILOT AND OWNER OF THE ELECTRA

MOVING THROUGH THE CLOUDS

HAVING FILMED WITH MIRA in many countries over the past nineteen years, it felt nothing less than perfect that we should find ourselves making a movie about a woman whose quest was to fly the circumference of the earth. We were immediately captivated as Amelia's story reflects our shared desires to discover new places, cross barriers, and to find inspiration through humanity, beauty, and freedom.

Our film family came together as we began to work first on the script with Anna Hamilton Phelan and the casting with Avy Kaufman. The definition of the visual landscape began with designer Stephanie Carroll and cinematographer Stuart Dryburgh working fearlessly with our visual effects supervisor, Wojciech Zielinski, to bring the real world, as photographed naturally, together with the design of the created visual effects. We built some of the planes, under the supervision of Paul Austerberry, and we also located authentic ones to fly, including the most glorious flying machine, the Lockheed Electra. Its design and beauty are beyond breathtaking. A veritable magic carpet in the early days of aviation. Our aerial coordinator, Marc Wolff created a ballet between the aerial camera and the Electra, yielding shots that defy any expectation one could possibly have.

As we worked on the development of Amelia's character with Anna, I came to identify with Amelia as a fierce competitor, a generous leader, and a woman of great imagination. As a young girl when her mother forbade her to ride the roller coaster at the county fair, she defiantly went home and built one of her own in her backyard. As an adult, she broke aviation records like a prizefighter, and she later used her success as a platform to champion the ERA and women's rights. When Amelia went on speaking tours promoting the first commercial airline venture, her iconic status was exemplified by the idea that if she could convince women to travel by air, the husbands would follow. These are some of the details that stay with me. Susan Butler's book, *East to the Dawn*, provided a comprehensive account of Amelia's extraordinary life. We also carried around dog-eared copies of Amelia's books, *For the Fun of It*, and *20 Hrs. 40 Min., Our Flight in the Friendship*.

During her time, Amelia represented hope and was an inspiration to people grappling with the deprivation and despair of the Great Depression. Ironically, we tell this story at a time when history has come around, with our present-day economy having crashed and our new president frequently likened to Franklin Roosevelt. Amelia inspires us now to step back from the rat race, help each other, and make time to dream.

Even though the word "tragic" is often used in connection with Amelia's death, I feel the spiritual poetry of the mystery of her disappearance, and her vital energy, is what we savor. Moving through the clouds, the orchestra and soulful piano of Gabriel Yared transports us with an elegance and a certain peace to the idea that she ultimately became one with the celestial spirits in her own inimitable style.

Lydia Dean Pilcher
PRODUCER

SS THE ATLANTIC

FIRST WOMAN TO CROSS THE ATLANTIC

TREPASSEY HARBOR, NEWFOUNDLAND, TO BURRY PORT, WALES, UNITED KINGDOM

JUNE 17, 1928

FOKKER F7 NAMED FRIENDSHIP

20 HRS 40 MIN

GEORGE Miss Earhart?

AMELIA Mr. Putnam?

GEORGE Please sit. I'm told you want to fly across the Atlantic Ocean.

AMELIA I do.

GEORGE Why do you want to fly?

AMELIA My dream has always been to fly across the Atlantic.

GEORGE Three women have died trying. Two others escaped with their lives. If you do make it, you'll be the first. Which...is the real attraction for both of us, I expect.

AMELIA Always nice to know what the real attraction is.

BILL What time is it?

> **AMELIA** It's time to fly. Get up, get dressed, we're going now.

BILL Where's the weather report?

> She goes to his bed. Hands him a slip of paper and opens the curtains.
> He blinks, still waking up. Reads.

BILL It's not good enough.

> **AMELIA** Great. Either we fly to Ireland or you're going home today.

BILL Well, it's—It's not good enough.

> **AMELIA** It's fine, there's a tail wind all the way, we'll off-load to 700
> gallons, which gets us off the water and the wind will get us to Ireland.

BILL You're dumping fuel? You're serious?

> **AMELIA** Just as serious as you're hung over. (to SLIM) Slim, you go now,
> get the late weather, we'll meet you at the plane.
>
> I've loved one person unconditionally, Bill. He is the most caring
> and generous and charming and flat-out funny guy I'll ever know.
> He's my father. Anyone would.
>
> He's a drunk. And he's let me down all my life. Now you get out
> of that god-damned bed. And you fly that plane to Ireland.
> Or I swear to you I will.

Amelia in the Friendship, 1928

AMELIA "I have often said that the lure of flying is the lure of beauty, and I need no other flight to convince me that the reason flyers fly, whether they know it or not, is the aesthetic appeal of flying."

BURRY PORT, WALES

SHERIFF Welcome!

AMELIA Thank you. Is it Irish tradition to- to greet newcomers with song?

SHERIFF I couldn't say. This is Wales!

Amelia, Bill Stultz, and Slim Gordon in Southampton, 1928

REPORTER #1 Are you proud to be the first woman to fly the Atlantic?

  AMELIA I was a passenger on this journey. Just a passenger. Everything that was done to bring us across was done by Wilmer Stultz and Slim Gordon. All the praise should—

REPORTER #2 But you can fly, can't you?

  AMELIA This flight was solely due to Bill and Slim. Women should know, however, that I have had 500 hours solo flying and certainly, one day a woman will do this.

It starts women thinking that there's more to life. Than being a passenger.

Ticker tape parade for
Amelia, 1932

Amelia at the parade, 1932

BREAKFAST ROOM, RYE

GEORGE I want you to marry me.

AMELIA I don't want to get married, George! I'm not the marrying kind.

GEORGE Don't you see? You and I embarking on a new life.

AMELIA Dear George—Only I can make a fulfilling life for myself.

GEORGE I don't believe one can have a fulfilled life alone. Only when it's shared...Let me share your life with you. Let me try to give you whatever you want.

AMELIA When I was a little girl...for my seventh birthday...my father gave me a globe. And I would spend hours just spinning it slowly...reading the names of all those strange, faraway places...Morocco...Spain, Africa. Dreaming that someday I would go to those places... like a wayfarer...a traveler...a vagabond.

I want to be free, George...To be a...vagabond of the air.

Noank
Connecticut

The Square House
Church Street

Dear GPP

        There are some things which should be writ before
we are married -- things we have talked over before -- most of
them.

        You must know again my reluctance to marry, my
feeling that I shatter thereby chances in work which means most
to me. I feel the move just now as foolish as anything I
could do. I know there may be compensations but have no heart
to look ahead.

        On our life together I want you to understand I
shall not hold you to any midaevil code of faithfulness to me
nor shall I consider myself bound to you similarly. If we can
be honest I think the difficulties which arise may best be avoided
should you or I become interested deeply (or inpassing) in anyone
else.

        Please let us not interfere with the others' work or
play, nor let the world see our private joys or disagreements.
In this connection I may have to keep some place where I can go to
be myself, now and then, for I cannot guarantee to endure at all
times the confinement of even an attractive cage.

        I must exact a cruel promise and that is you will let
me go in a year if we find no happiness together.

        I will try to do my best in every way and give you that
part of me you know and seem to want.

                                A.E.

Amelia's letter to
George Putnam, 1931

Amelia and George, 1935

MINISTER Amelia, do you promise to love, honor and obey…

AMELIA Excuse me, Sir. May we take that back a bit, please. "Love," yes, if it's warranted. "Honor," same thing. "Obey?" I can't promise that under any circumstances. But the groom understands that.

GEORGE Please remove "obey" from the prayer so we can wrap this up… before the bride runs off.

DINING ROOM, RYE

AMELIA George? I've been thinking.

GEORGE Yes?

AMELIA I want to fly the Atlantic.

GEORGE You already have.

AMELIA As a passenger. It doesn't count. I want to fly it solo.

GEORGE It's been five years since Lindbergh. No one has made it solo. Fourteen have died trying.

AMELIA I'll make it. I know I will.

GEORGE And if you don't?

AMELIA I'd rather face a watery grave than go on living as a fraud.

GEORGE What's wrong with that? I've been very successful at it.

Amelia and George, 1935

TRANSITIONS

MUCH LIKE AMELIA'S own journey, the experience of editing the film was one of adventure and serendipity. In February we all felt we were very close to being finished, but due to scheduling issues we took a brief hiatus. This turned out to be a stroke of luck, because in stepping back we were able to see the film with a clarity that simply wasn't possible when we were deep into it on a daily basis. Perhaps it was because Mira Nair is a yogi, but the distance gave us perspective, and we realized that there were completely unexplored possibilities in the footage.

The story was being told following the chronology of Amelia's life. This meant we needed certain scenes and details to logically move the story from one event to the next. We realized that by structuring the film as an extension of Amelia's experience during her final flight around the world, we would be able to put the viewer into her head and eliminate scenes that provided little more than continuity. Each day in the editing

room became a tumble of ideas. Scenes would be eliminated and often weeks later reinstated, but in a different place and with a different structure, thereby becoming more meaningful than they had originally been.

We found we would rush to the editing room each morning with the enthusiasm of students learning a new language. And every time we thought we were finished we'd watch the movie with our friends, producers, and executives only to unearth new possibilities. Our journey wasn't a direct one, but the film comes closer to the feeling Amelia has when flying—memories come and go, without chronology—like dreams.

Lee Percy
EDITOR

CLEVELAND AIRFIELD

ANNOUNCER Here they come, folks! In first place: Louise Thaden from Bentonville, Arkansas. In second place: Gladys O'Donnell from Long Beach, California. Third place goes to Amelia Earhart, Atchison, Kansas.

REPORTER How does it feel to finish third?

AMELIA Oh, a victory for any woman flyer is a victory for me. I'd like to add my congratulations to Louise Thaden. And announce that we have formed an organization to promote women in aviation. 99 women pilots have applied, so we're calling it the 99's. And we're going to make a difference!

Amelia with race contestants, 1934

Amelia making a speech, 1929

Amelia parachuting, 1935

NORTHERN IRELAND

NEWFOUNDLAND

F I R S T W O M A N T O F L Y S O

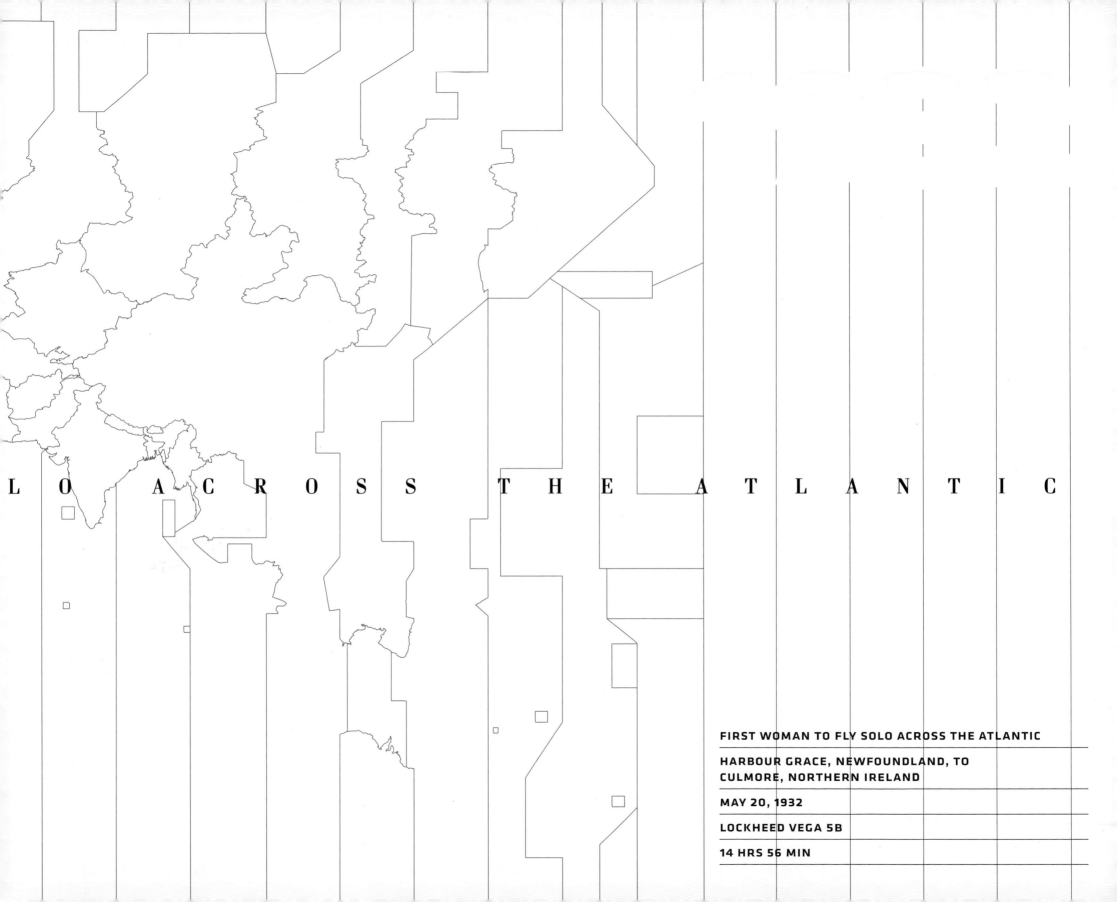

LO ACROSS THE ATLANTIC

FIRST WOMAN TO FLY SOLO ACROSS THE ATLANTIC

HARBOUR GRACE, NEWFOUNDLAND, TO
CULMORE, NORTHERN IRELAND

MAY 20, 1932

LOCKHEED VEGA 5B

14 HRS 56 MIN

VEGA

WEATHERMAN (V.O.) Presently all clear on the Atlantic. Keeping an eye on a storm system south of the route.

AMELIA (V.O.) It was a night of stars. Of tropic loveliness. Stars hung outside my cockpit window near enough to touch.

Amelia in Ireland, 1932

NORTHERN IRELAND

AMELIA Excuse me, sir. Where am I?

MAN In Gallagher's pasture. Where are ya supposed to be?

AMELIA When I left, I was aiming for Paris.

MAN Ya missed, y'know. (points) It's over there.

PUSHING FORWARD

MIRA CREATED her own vocabulary when she would refer to this section as "the commodification montage"—but it made perfect sense. After all, it is believed that George Putnam was the first man who truly invented public relations, as we now know it, making Amelia one of the first celebrities to endorse all sorts of products.

Mira Nair asked me to work on previous films as a yoga instructor for the cast and crew. For this movie Mira asked me to create a "yogic ballet" for this "commodification" idea. We joked about having "babes" do headstands on the wings of a plane. When I arrived on location and saw the fabulous sets, beautifully crafted props, and stunning costumes, I felt like I had been transported to the time when Amelia was flying.

The challenge came with having six different sections, with very limited time, on a very tight schedule—one day to rehearse and one day to shoot! It became a yoga practice for me: focus, concentrate, and solve the problems. I also had to practice nonattachment as I knew most of what I would come up with would probably not get used, but I also wanted to have

enough options to show Mira so she could choose what she liked best.

The "babes" that I worked with were all gorgeous beauties and real troopers! We had to rehearse in one place where the ceiling was too low to raise the globes over their heads, so they ended up practicing a whole section on their knees, and they never complained. It was only during a break when they all had ice packs on their knees that I was aware that they had been silently suffering. As I watched these strong young women at work, and observed Mira directing this massive project, I found myself thinking about the example that Amelia set as an incredibly independent and strong woman, pushing forward to achieve her goals no matter what obstacles lay in her path.

Mira, like Amelia, is a strong woman who once she sets her mind on something doesn't give up. Working around Mira has always been an inspiration and this time I had the privileged of being part of the creative process.

James Murphy
CHOREOGRAPHER

CONSTITUTIONAL HALL BACKSTAGE

AMELIA Here I am jumping through hoops like a white horse in the circus...That's what's wrong.

    GEORGE The only way we can finance your flying is to make enough money to finance your flying.

ANNOUNCER Tonight we have the real pleasure of presenting the second human to fly the Atlantic solo, the only one to ever fly it twice. Ladies and gentleman, AMELIA EARHART!

    GEORGE Now go on out there.

AMELIA takes a deep breath and goes "out there." She's already playing to the cameras downstage, left.

AMELIA Thank you. Thank you very much.

CONSTITUTIONAL HALL STAIRS

AMELIA Oh, God, do I have to wade through that?

GENE You have two Vidal men protecting you. You'll be fine.

"Anything which tends to annihilate distance destroys isolation, and brings the world and its peoples closer together. I think aviation has a chance to increase intimacy, understanding, and far-flung friendship thus."

Amelia Earhart, 1928

Amelia in London, 1928

OAKLAND

HONOLULU

FIRST PERSON TO CRO

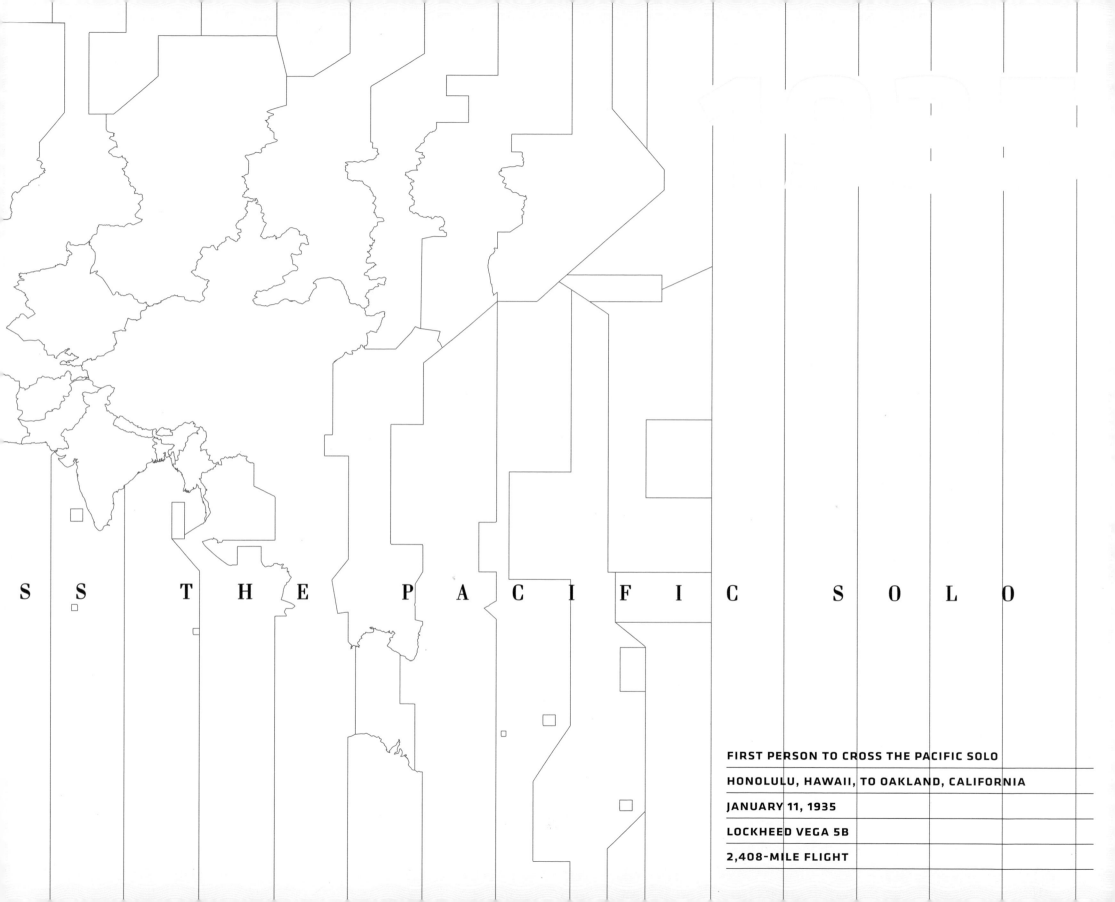

SS THE PACIFIC SOLO

FIRST PERSON TO CROSS THE PACIFIC SOLO

HONOLULU, HAWAII, TO OAKLAND, CALIFORNIA

JANUARY 11, 1935

LOCKHEED VEGA 5B

2,408-MILE FLIGHT

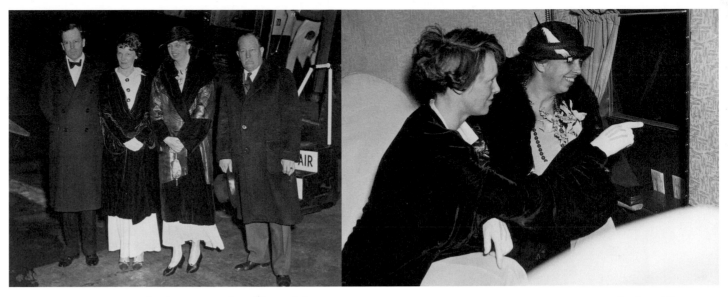

George, Amelia, Eleanor Roosevelt, and Thomas B. Doe, 1933

Amelia and Eleanor, 1933

BANQUET HALL, WASHINGTON, D.C.

ELEANOR Your husband encourages you to fly across the Atlantic.
My husband wouldn't want me to fly to N Street.

> **AMELIA** So he hasn't actually forbidden you.

ELEANOR Franklin doesn't forbid. He just feels it's a waste of my valuable time to
learn. Since I can't afford to buy a plane.

> **AMELIA** The wrong Roosevelt got elected.

ELEANOR I did ask about aviation, but he hasn't decided on the structure yet.
It might be under the Bureau of Commerce.

> **AMELIA** I think the structure may be less important than the man
> chosen to run it.

ELEANOR I'm sorry, my hearing is failing. I missed the words 'or woman?'

> **AMELIA** This may be one of those rare instances. When the most
> accomplished candidate. Turns out to be male.

ELEANOR I love finding the exception that proves the rule.

> **AMELIA** How do you feel about flying at night?

AMELIA'S COSTUMES

THE PROCESS OF designing costumes for Amelia was full of fun. The mere mention of her name sparked creativity and enthusiasm.

Amelia herself had an amazing range of looks—from flying wear and greasy coveralls to casual day looks to very glamorous evening dresses. She loved clothes, and during our research we discovered hundreds of variations of shirts, scarves, jackets, and dresses. Sometimes our re-creations were almost exact, while others were but an approximation of styles and looks.

We start with her as a young social worker (at which time she already owned two furs), and later explore her custom-made garments that showed sophisticated simplicity with exquisite details—like french cuffs on work shirts. Amelia channeled her sense of style into her own luggage and clothing lines.

The challenge came as we searched for the stocks to dress four thousand people as background characters. Between the costume houses, several vintage vendors, flea market searches, and extensive tailoring, we pulled it off. Our Toronto crew was extraordinary in making the clothing come to life.

In *East to the Dawn*, Susan Butler wrote, "Amelia worked at her image. Just as her hair seemed artless, so her clothes, her look, presented a consistent image of understatement and casualness that was deliberate...Her seeming casualness was deceptive. The functional slacks were custom made, perfectly tailored... in her public appearances—she made a point to dress conservatively and yet with her style—to look the very best to her audience, to appear as someone whom the men and women listening would accept as their social equal, someone with their values."

The discovery of her character, the great spirit of the movie team, and our far-reaching travels made for a real adventure.

Kasia Walicka Maimone
COSTUME DESIGNER

RESTAURANT, BOSTON

GENE Transcontinental was too ambitious. Too many hops, too tough on the ladies. But the shuttle... Washington, New York, Boston. We think it's the future. Will you go there with us?

AMELIA What on earth would you need me for?

PAUL You are the most famous woman in America, that's what for...You know, I can see it now... You on the poster with Gene. A legendary athlete at West Point, two events at the Olympics, a top pilot who's going to be running the skies for Roosevelt–

GENE Thanks, Paul. I think you've even talked me out of it.

INT. SAME—BAR—LATER

GENE May I ask you a question?

　AMELIA That woman over there. She's beautiful.

GENE You're the only woman I know who points out other beautiful women.

　AMELIA Lovely legs...unlike mine.

GENE Now I'm sure that's not true. That's why you wear trousers?

　AMELIA nods.

GENE No. And all this while I thought you just wanted to be one of the boys.

　AMELIA I may have, at one time. But not anymore.

Gene Vidal and Amelia, ca. 1930

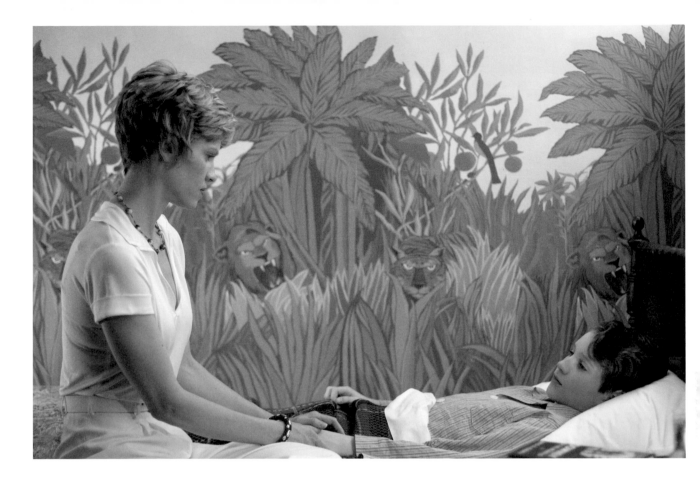

GUEST ROOM

AMELIA It's okay. Do you know why I papered this room like this?

GORE No. But I wish you hadn't.

AMELIA It's because I'm very, very afraid of jungles. So when I find myself worrying about it, I test my courage by coming into this room and pretending I'm in the deepest, darkest part of Africa. In a jungle so thick I can't even see the sky above. And I start to feel better right away because I looked my fear right in the face.

PUTNAM'S OFFICE

AMELIA Hello.

GEORGE I found something you'd written. Quite beautiful.

We see a hand-written poem addressed to "Dearest Gene":
"To touch your hand, and see your face today is joy. Your casual presence in a room recalls the stars that watched us as we lay. I mark you in the moving crowd, and see again those stars a warm night lent us long ago. We loved so then, we love so now."

AMELIA At the time I...George...

GEORGE hangs up phone. AMELIA'S eyes fill with tears.

AMELIA George...

GEORGE I want you to give me something…tell me this is your last record flight.

AMELIA How can we be anything but what we are?

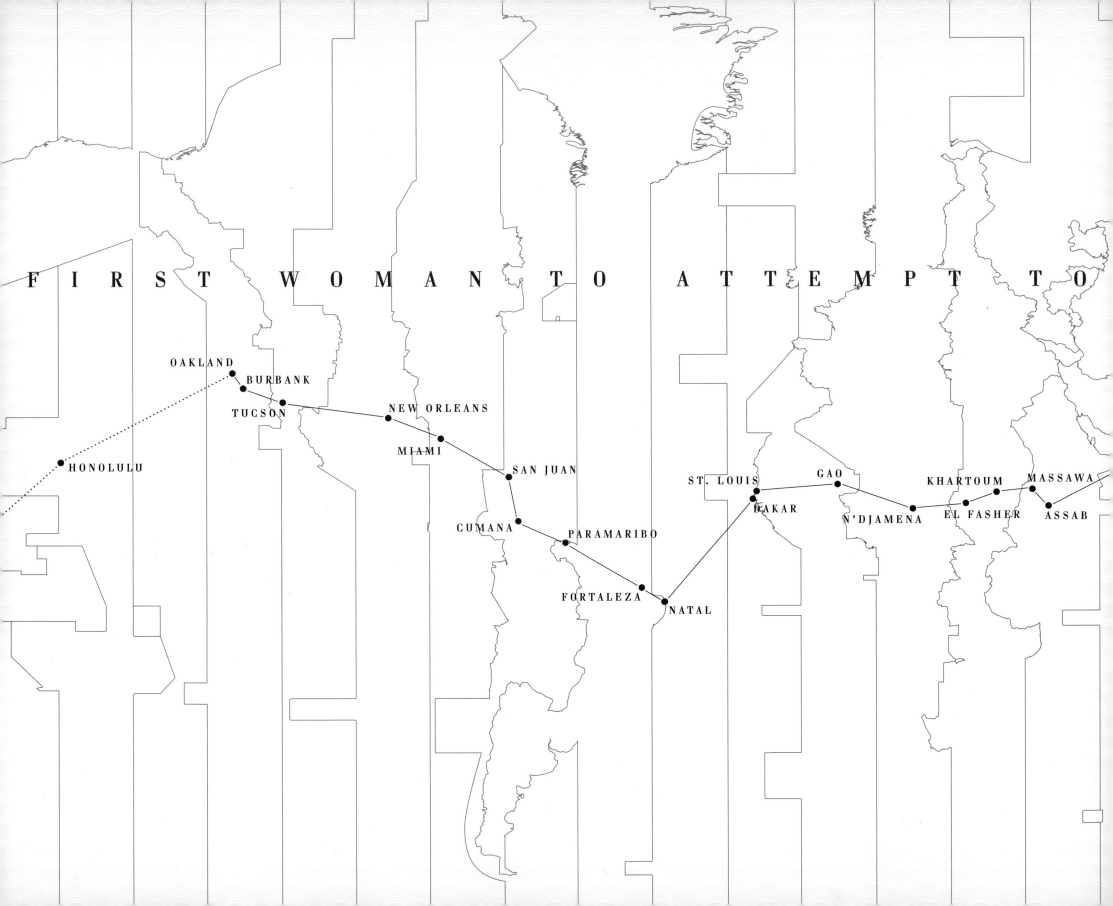

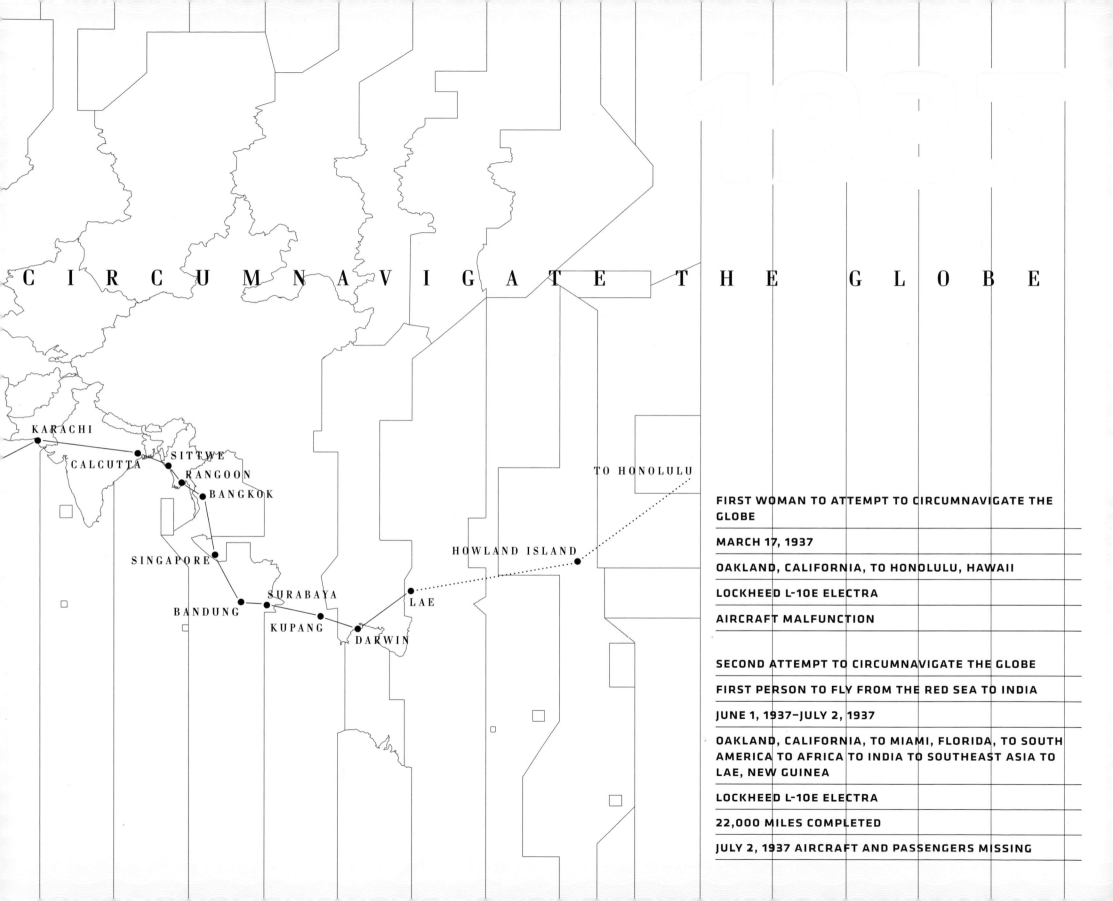

CIRCUMNAVIGATE THE GLOBE

KARACHI

CALCUTTA SITTWE
RANGOON
BANGKOK

TO HONOLULU

SINGAPORE

HOWLAND ISLAND

SURABAYA
BANDUNG
KUPANG
DARWIN
LAE

FIRST WOMAN TO ATTEMPT TO CIRCUMNAVIGATE THE GLOBE

MARCH 17, 1937

OAKLAND, CALIFORNIA, TO HONOLULU, HAWAII

LOCKHEED L-10E ELECTRA

AIRCRAFT MALFUNCTION

SECOND ATTEMPT TO CIRCUMNAVIGATE THE GLOBE

FIRST PERSON TO FLY FROM THE RED SEA TO INDIA

JUNE 1, 1937–JULY 2, 1937

OAKLAND, CALIFORNIA, TO MIAMI, FLORIDA, TO SOUTH AMERICA TO AFRICA TO INDIA TO SOUTHEAST ASIA TO LAE, NEW GUINEA

LOCKHEED L-10E ELECTRA

22,000 MILES COMPLETED

JULY 2, 1937 AIRCRAFT AND PASSENGERS MISSING

GEORGE If you're serious about this flying around-the-world nonsense, it might be handy to have a plane to fly in.

AMELIA Except it would have to be an Electra, and they cost...

GEORGE ...$36,000. After a generous discount from Lockheed.

AMELIA May as well be a billion.

GEORGE ...not to mention at least another 36 to have it modified and ready.

AMELIA And your surprise is, you robbed a bank.

GEORGE Well, actually. A university. I've persuaded Ed Elliot to create an Amelia Earhart Fund for Aeronautical Research at Purdue. And suggested a budget amount of...

...eighty thousand dollars. For a suitable 'flying laboratory.'

AMELIA The Electra?

GEORGE Your Electra, Amelia.

A. E.'s 'Flying Laboratory' Purdue Based

SOME critics, without bothering to check facts, dubbed Amelia Earhart's 1937 global plans the "just for fun" flight. Others, jumping to an erroneous conclusion, howled about state funds being used to purchase the $80,000 "flying laboratory," a twin-engine Lockheed Electra.

Neither charge was true. The flight was no whim. Rather, it was carefully planned. Behind it was a desire for knowledge—Miss Earhart was interested in pilot fatigue, food consumption and the performance of her radio, engine and fuel. The scientific information that she would collect was to have been "placed in the hands of the Department of Aeronautics."

The slim aviatrix with the wind-blown hair said: "The information I bring back may be valuable or it may not; the important thing is to keep an open mind."

★ ★ ★

At a dinner party given by Dr. Edward C. Elliott, president of Purdue University, Miss

IN this $80,000 "flying laboratory," a twin-engine Lockheed Electra, Miss Earhart and her navigator, Capt. Fred Noonan, were lost in the Pacific on July 2, 1937. The plane (cruising speed 190 mph) was built on the west coast then brought to Purdue, where Miss Earhart wrapped all the gas and oil lines to prevent leakage. For her global flight, fuel was spotted at over 30 spots along her course.

Earhart was asked by J. K. Lilly, a trustee, what she planned to do next. She broached the idea of the around-the-world flight. Lilly offered $20,000, a figure matched by David E. Ross, president of the Purdue board. Eventually about $100,000 was raised and given to the Purdue Research Foundation for the purchase of the Electra.

The plane was one of the best equipped of the day. Miss Earhart personally checked installation of instruments in the NR16020.

Miss Earhart covered 20,000 miles . . . then disappeared somewhere between Lae and Howland Island in July. Later that month she would have been 39.

Her husband, G. P. Putnam, wrote Purdue officials: "The best opinion of those close to the whole tragic circumstance is that the plane probably crashed on hitting the water and everything was over quickly."

"Please know I am quite aware of the hazards of the trip. I want to do it because I want to do it. Women must try to do things as men have tried. When they fail, their failure must be a challenge to others."

IN MARCH, 1937, Miss Earhart made her first attempt to circle the globe in the Electra, but a tire blew out on takeoff at Luke Field Hawaii. By immediately switching off the engines, she avoided a fire. The plane was shipped back to the States where it was repaired. She then reversed the direction of her 27,000-mile flight, taking off from Miami, June 1.

WITH Wiley Post, Col. Roscoe Turner and Laura Ingalls.

Photos Courtesy of Purdue Libraries

UPPER LEFT: In the Purdue libraries display are her flying suit and helmet. Her husband gave the university h u n d r e d s of photographs, lecture programs, personal letters. (Staff Photo)

THE aviatrix holds a Bendix direction finder with w h i c h the Electra was fitted in addition to a Sperry gyro pilot and a two-way voice and telegraph radio communications system.

THE JOURNAL AND COURIER, LAFAYETTE, IND.

July 20, 1942, Page 2

XII. A. 1.

Amelia in the cockpit of the Electra, ca. 1936

NEWSCASTER

AMELIA EARHART LEAVES OAKLAND FOR HONOLULU,
SETTING OUT ON THE MOST DANGEROUS AERONAUTIC
FEAT EVER ATTEMPTED TO TRAVERSE THE WAISTLINE
OF THE WORLD. FROM PARIS TO PERU COME WISHES OF:
GODSPEED AMELIA!

Amelia on the nose of the Electra, 1937

"I think my husband has always found a sort of grim satisfaction—a species of modern martyrdom—in being, for once, the male left behind while the female fares forth adventure-bound, thus turning topsy-turvy the accepted way of the world in such matters."

Amelia Earhart, 1937

FRED Pan Am told you I'm the best celestial navigator they've ever seen.

AMELIA They did.

FRED Someone else told you I got a drinking problem. Which is a big part of why we're here, right? Everyone I ever worked for will tell you. Nothing's interfered with my performance. Not once.

AMELIA You'd be looking for an island less than two miles long, with nothing higher on it than 18 feet.

FRED That's what you'd be looking for. I'd be looking for coordinates on a map.

AMELIA How can I lose?

Amelia and Fred Noonan, 1937

Amelia and George saying
goodbye, 1937

AIRFIELD

AMELIA Clear!

AMELIA ROARS OFF, gathering SPEED. The Electra SUDDENLY VEERS TO THE RIGHT, and we SMASH CUT TO...

AMELIA THROTTLING DOWN the left engine. The plane SWINGING WILDLY to the left, as...the RIGHT WHEEL COLLAPSES, the plane SPINS TO THE LEFT and we INTERCUT between the cockpit and the runway as the Electra...CAREENS MADLY for a thousand feet, AMELIA CUTTING THE SWITCHES to the engines, fighting for control, PROPELLERS SMASHED by the concrete runway, SPARKS FLYING IN EVERY DIRECTION...

SMASH CUT to the cockpit, the Electra SPINNING crazily on its belly, SPARKS EVERYWHERE, the plane suddenly comes...to a BONE-JARRING STOP. The right MOTOR is pushed up INTO its wing, which itself has BUCKLED, the stabilizer BENT, the left wing extends UPWARD from scraping the runway, the landing gear no longer exists. SIRENS SCREAM as fire trucks and ambulances race toward them. AMELIA is ashen, disbelieving. Next to her, a gentle...

AMELIA You alright?!

FRED Good reaction, cutting the switch. You saved our ass!

BEDROOM—LOS ANGELES HOME

AMELIA I'll make it good, GP, I swear to you I will. I'll make it back and more, I promise. The book sales, the lectures, this flight will keep us going another three years.

GEORGE Maybe.

AMELIA No, it will, I promise. Our sales, our prices, are going to double. This showed them how dangerous it all is, they were taking it for granted... They thought I was competent.

GEORGE I meant. Or maybe we can just stop.

AMELIA You mean after.

GEORGE Or. Even now.

AMELIA So my exit would be a stupid crash. And withdrawing from a world-publicized attempt to finally do something no man had done before. It would ruin us, the bargain. We'd have nothing.

GEORGE Uh-huh. It's true. And I'd be fine with that.

AMELIA That's because you're an idiot.

GEORGE Lucky for you.

AMELIA And what if it's not something I need to show the world? What if it's something I need to show me?

AMELIA THE LEGEND

EVERYONE KNOWS of Amelia Earhart, but few really know anything about Amelia Earhart. That's what really inspired me to make this movie. The more I researched her life, the more inspired I became.

Her sheer guts, passion, drive, and refusal to let barriers stand in her way left an indelible impression on me. She was a trailblazer for women, and became a true pioneer in a man's world. She set the standard highest for herself, and raised the bar for everyone around her and everyone who would follow after her death. She broke the rules, and rewrote them when she didn't like them. From her marriage to her record-breaking flights, she was never content with the status quo.

In an era when some people have forgotten about the risks people took in previous generations to enable our current freedoms, I hope this film inspires someone to take risks, to enable a better future for our next generations. Amelia Earhart risked her life over and over again to make the world a better place. Her death made her a legend, but it's her life we could all learn from.

Ted Waitt
PRODUCER

"...Africa to me was a riot of human color...Tall black figures endowed with a certain innate dignity went about their own affairs...Seeing the majesty of these natives I asked myself what many must have asked before: What have we in the United States done to these proud people, so handsome and intelligent in the setting of their own country?"

Amelia Earhart, 1937

Amelia on a camel, 1937

AMELIA If you have a point, make it.

FRED I believe I have.

AMELIA All you need to do is just show up tomorrow morning, show up sober.
And get me to Howland Island.

GEORGE After the Fourth. We're going home.

AMELIA Where's that?

GEORGE For me? Anywhere you are.

AMELIA I'm going to like it there.
I'd better. Since this is going to be my last flight.

GEORGE If you insist.

AMELIA I love you.

AMELIA Should I let you go now?

GEORGE Never...I'll go tell the world you're on your way.

AMELIA See ya. My darling.

GEORGE See ya. My love.

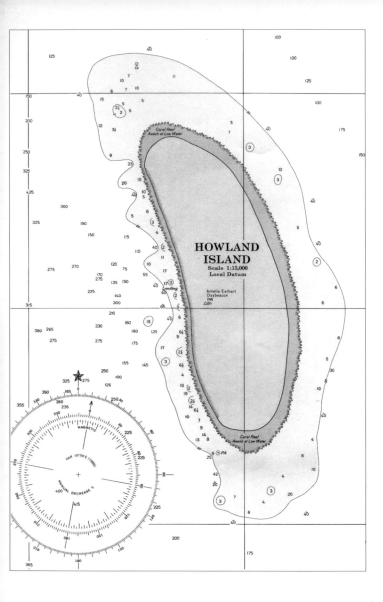

RADIO ROOM

AMELIA (O.S.) ITASCA this is KING HOWELL ABEL QUEEN QUEEN. We must be on you but cannot see you...

Fuel is running low. Been unable to receive you by radio. We are flying at altitude 1000 feet. Over.

> **DALTEN** We are receiving you and transmitting on 3105 and 500 consistently. Over.

AMELIA can't hear anything, bangs microphone in frustration.

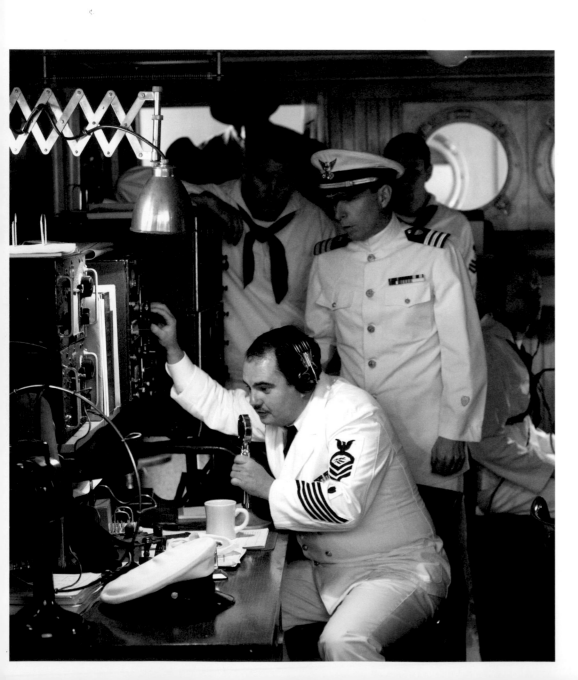

RADIO ROOM (CONT'D)

AMELIA (O.S.) Itasca, we are circling but cannot hear you. Over.

BELLARTS King Howell Abel Queen Queen, this is Itasca. Your signal is strong. Are you receiving this? Over.

A breathless moment. A sharp CRACKLE.

AMELIA (O.S.) Itasca this is King Howell Abel Queen Queen. We received your signal, but unable to take a bearing. Please take bearing on us and answer 3105 with voice. Over.

BELLARTS Your signal received okay. It is impossible to take a bearing on 3105 on your voice. Send us a longer transmission please. Over.

Silence. Feet are shifting. No one speaks.

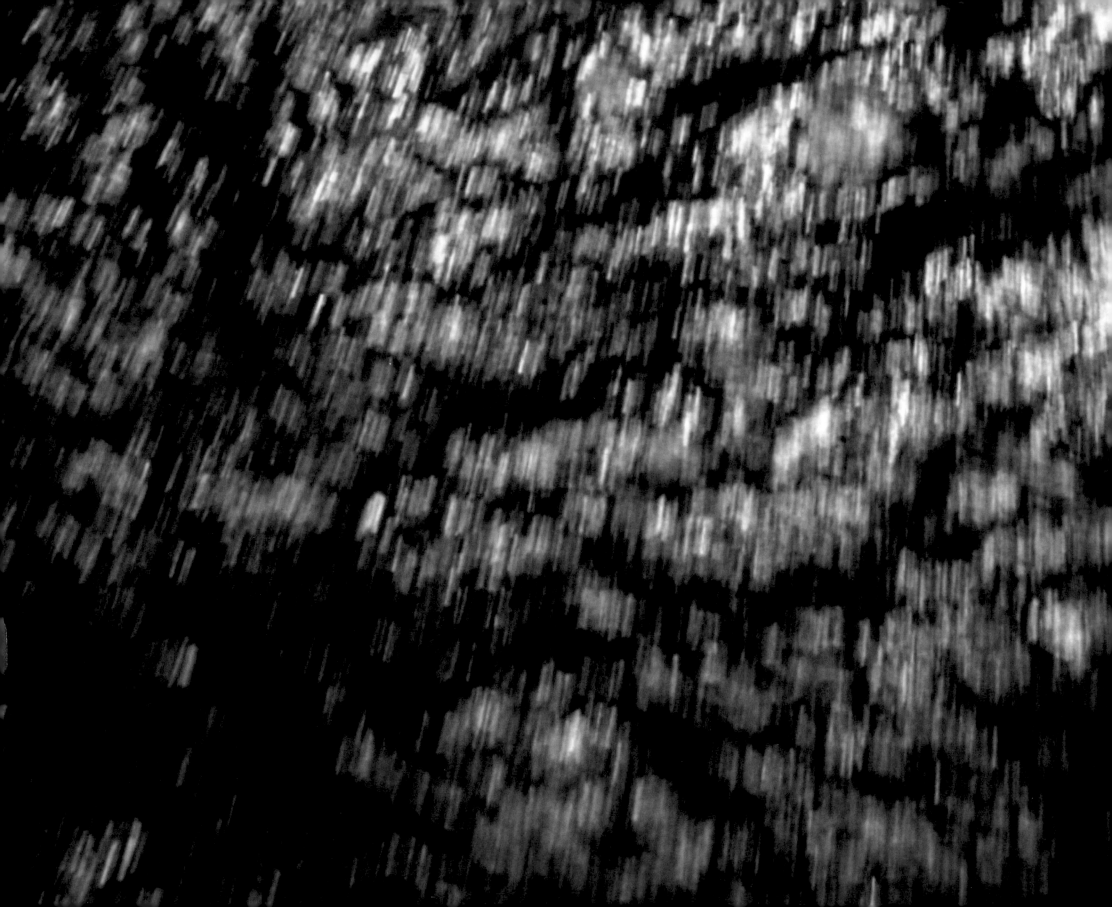

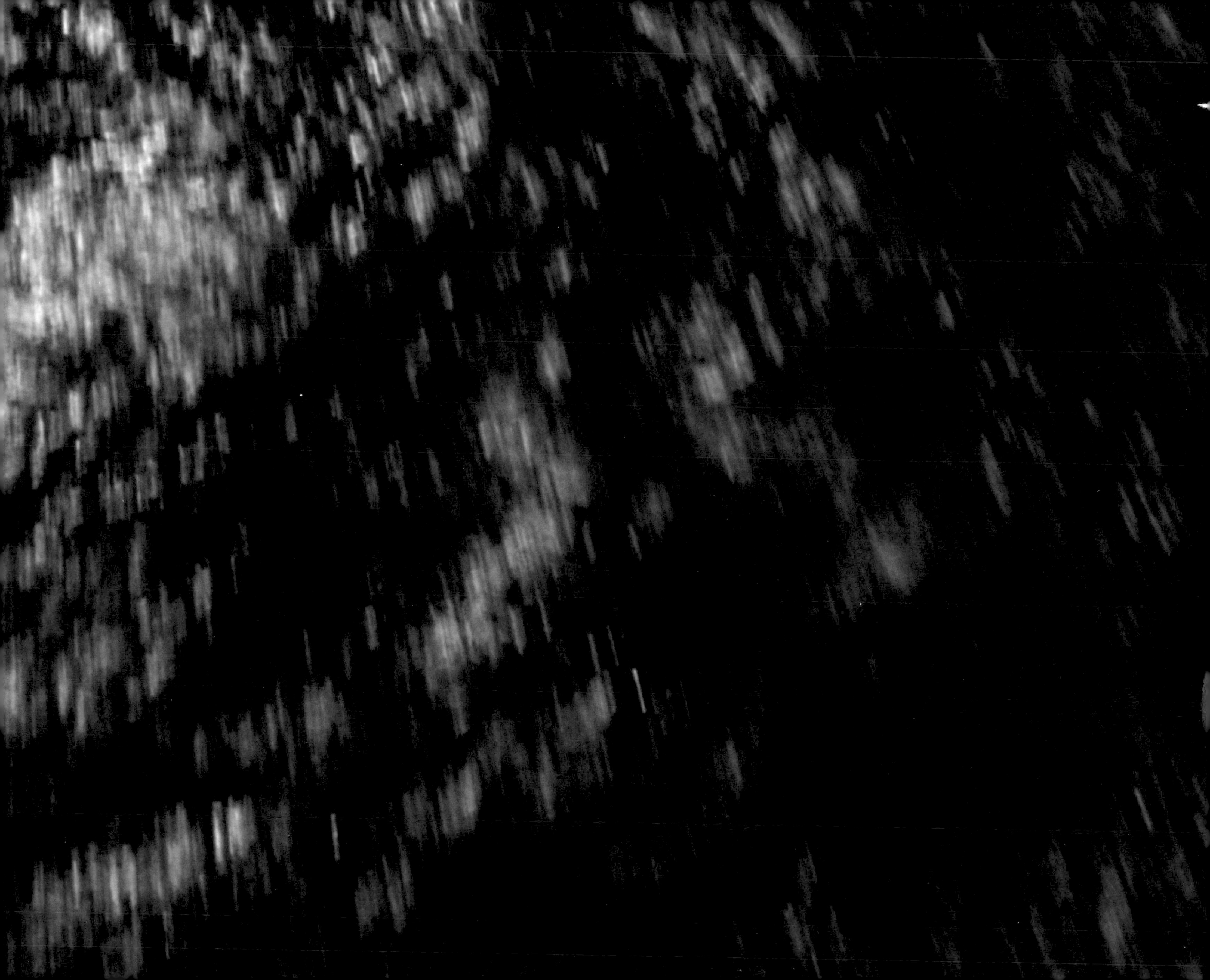

COAST GUARD STATION, LOS ANGELES

AMELIA (v.o.) All the things I never said for so very long, look up—they're in my eyes.

When I'm flying upward toward the sun, I feel transported somehow to a simple, safe, beautiful place where everything is comprehensible.

A huge thank you to our book design team, the great Abbott Miller and his right hand, Susan Brzozowski, who made Amelia soar. I would like to acknowledge Lydia Dean Pilcher for making sure this book happened properly, Ken Woroner for taking many of these splendid photographs, Caitlin McFarland, Christine McKeever, and Dhruv Vasishtha for pulling it all together, and our brilliant cast and crew who gave the film their all.

Mira Nair

First published in the
United States of America in 2009 by
Universe Publishing,
A Division of Rizzoli International
Publications, Inc.
300 Park Avenue South
New York, NY 10010
www.rizzoliusa.com

™ and © 2009 Twentieth Century
Fox Film Corporation.

2009 2010 2011 2012 / 10 9 8 7 6 5 4 3 2 1

Design: Abbott Miller, Susan Brzozowski
Pentagram
Printed in the United States of America

ISBN-13: 978-0-7893-1840-4

Library of Congress Catalog Control
Number: 2009931664

PHOTO CREDITS

Archival images on pages 4, 12, 38, 40, 58, 59, 77, 107, and 143
© Bettmann/CORBIS

Childhood photograph on page 5
Courtesy Mira Nair

Archival photographs and documents on pages 10, 36, 44, 81, 89, 99, 100, 101, 105, and 120
From the George Palmer Putnam Collection of the Amelia Earhart Papers, courtesy of Purdue University Libraries, Karnes Archives & Special Collections

Archival photographs on pages 30 and 67
The New York Times Photo Archives

Archival photograph on page 46
From the Schlesinger Library, Radcliffe Institute, Harvard University

Archival photograph on page 48
Unidentified Photographer
Amelia Earhart and George Palmer Putnam, September 16, 1935.
© AP/Worldwide Photos, courtesy International Center of Photography, The Life Magazine Collection

Archival photograph on page 65
"The Society's Special Medal Awarded to Amelia Earhart," National Geographic, September 1932.
© Staff / National Geographic Image Collection, courtesy International Center of Photography

Costume sketches on page 82
Courtesy of Kasia Walicka Maimone, illustrated by Sandra Spannan

Map on page 128
Courtesy of www.britishempire.co.uk

Amelia Earhart, ca. 1930